Diary of a Brazilian Waxer

KIM GIDER

Year of the Book
135 Glen Avenue
Glen Rock, PA 17327

Print ISBN: 978-1-949150-97-1
Ebook ISBN: 978-1-64649-000-4

Illustrations by Jennifer Errickson

In Memory of

My beautiful mother,
Darlene Candelet Mirijanian

Special Thanks to

Bill Paugh, Demi Stevens, and Jennifer Errickson

Contents

Introduction

Hi! I'm Kim Gider, licensed esthetician and owner of Salon and Spa by Kimberly Gider in Conshohocken, Pennsylvania, right near the city of brotherly love. I have received numerous accolades and awards for my waxing talents. I decided to write this book to share my trials and tribulations with you.

I can't wait to fill you in with all my crazy stories! Waxing can be scary. A little painful, yes, but a skilled esthetician knows how to get the job done quickly and efficiently.

I am a very blunt person, as you will soon find out. I tell it like it is, and don't care what other people think.

*If you are easily offended,
put this book down now!*

If words like vagina, crotch, cooch, ass, or boobs make you feel uncomfortable, then this is not the book for you.

A seasoned waxee will thank me for unveiling this secret behind-the-scenes world. A waxing virgin will hopefully have the balls to go get that bush whacked after reading this book.

Some of you have probably been scarred for life from getting waxed in the backroom of some dirty nail salon for five bucks. Trust me, what I'm about to tell you is the real deal. This book will make you laugh your ass off and will also provide firsthand insight into the wonderful world of waxing.

If words like vagina, crotch, cooch, ass, and boobs make you feel uncomfortable, then this is not the book for you.

A crotch is a crotch is a crotch. I've seen thousands and nothing fazes me anymore. My clients and friends tell me they're afraid of being judged after I see their vagina. Ninety-nine percent of the time, all I see is the hair that needs to be removed. A good esthetician focuses on removing your pubic hair so that you leave with clean, bare, beautiful skin. Now as for the other one percent of the time, well... *let me explain...*

Once you get waxed, you'll never go back!

Okay, here we go. For those of you who have never been waxed "down there," get over your fear of the process. You have no idea the clean feel of smooth, silky skin in your privates. Forget the razor stubble or the drugstore creams. No one wants to put their hands or face on a bearded crotch!

The feeling of clean permeates under your jeans the minute you pull up your panties. Clean, clean, clean is how you'll feel. There is no other way to explain this sensation. Once your man (or woman) gets a look at what you've done, they'll be begging you to do this forevermore.

Ladies, just a little hint – tell your lover it would be really sexy to receive a fat, juicy gift card for your next couple of waxes. Hot lingerie included with that gift card makes the perfect bundle!

Once you get waxed, you'll wonder how in the f*%# you lived all these years with that nasty disaster down there. The '70s are over. Throw those grannies away. Now it's time to play!

Underneath it all

People come in thinking that a bikini, Brazilian, or whatever wax is so mysterious. I'm going to let the cat out of the bag here, people: waxing is me ripping and tugging the hair out of your skin. There's no foreplay, no bells, no whistles, just warm wax placed where it has to be, with a rice paper strip pulling out those stubborn pubes. Are you excited about this? Now, do I have your attention?

Guys and gals approach me all the time with feelings of shame about getting waxed. I just tell them, "I'm not going to take you to dinner or kiss you. Drop your pants and undies and let's get the show on the road."

People who come in for the first time usually have that "deer in the headlights" look on their faces, but leave with smiles from here to kingdom come. You might be a little sore or even slightly bruised after your virgin wax, but in just a few days, you'll be ready to jump back on that saddle again.

Just remember what I told you earlier – a trained, licensed esthetician like myself won't dissect your crotch looking for imperfections. I'm not no dungeon dom, ogre, or boxer. Just here to get the job done, and wrestle those legs open.

Let's get one thing straight: you don't have to be a red-carpet Kardashian to strip that mound of hair down there.

Remember this. When getting your wax, don't just lay there with your legs squeezed shut and expect me to crowbar and chisel my way to your vagenitals. Spread those legs wide open.

Your waxer observes the hair and can't do the job unless you are fully spread eagle. Don't be embarrassed to throw those legs up in the air and let me get every last hair. Clenching together like you're holding a jellybean in your ass, won't allow me to do my best work. It's not weird to me, seeing you spread your ass cheeks out for the world to see. Let me at it, bitch!

Take it off, baby!

Please, please, please take it off! When I say 'take it off,' I mean take *everything* off. Delusional first-timers lay down, pull their underwear over, and expect me just to remove the sides. Meanwhile, they know they have an overgrown bush. No way, Jose. We're not in Kansas anymore. The caveman look went out decades ago. Let's shape it up! Make it look decent down there.

My suggestion to people is to let me trim a bit, and they still insist for me just to clean the sides. Girlfriend, do you want your man to call the local exterminator? If all you want is clean sides, make sure you wear a sarong over that bathing suit 'cause there's definitely gonna be some creepy crawlers coming out of the sides. Spiders are not attractive. People are scared of them for a reason. Take it all off.

Like Nike says, "JUST DO IT!"

Call 911 – We've Got a Bleeder!

OMG. After you read this you're going to be like, "Oh no, she didn't!" Imagine this scenario. A client comes in, lays on the table, and we start the wax. I pull her legs up and... whoops! Guess we didn't know that Mother Nature was knocking on this glorious day.

The spillage begins and the client asks, "Oh, am I bleeding?" What did you think, bitch? You know you had cramps this morning so don't play yourself. The hell with your bullshit about thinking your period was over "like" today. You just got blood all over my beautifully crisp white sheet. Oxi clean, here we come. Unfortunately Billy Mays is deceased because I'd like to see him get this freaking blood stain out during his million-dollar commercial.

Don't act like you don't know you're bleeding all over. A word of advice – if Aunt Flo is in town, either reschedule your appointment or wear a clean tampon before entering the waxing zone. I stress, *clean* tampon, because no one (especially me), wants to look at that bloody, clotty, nasty ass string. Like the English say, "Bloody hell!"

OMG! Where's the Air Freshener?! (What a Douche!)

I'm a woman so I get it. Sometimes it gets pretty funky down there. If you know you're going to get waxed, wash it, spray it, whatever, but please make sure when certain parts open wide that I don't pass out at the bedside. Here I go rhyming again.

Ladies, no one wants to smell your stench from the gym, office, or all-day car ride. If you don't want to shower daily, it's your choice, but on appointment day, wash up your vajayjay.

Don't act like you can't smell yourself. Every woman knows when they smell like a fresh can of tuna. Please don't spoil my appetite with your stench. Show up with a clean cooch so we can begin the process without me wearing a gas mask.

Girl, there's something called flushable wipes.

1. Clean your front area... well.
2. Clean your back area... well.
3. And I mean *well*.

Congratulations, you're ready for your wax. You've just graduated from Wiping 101.

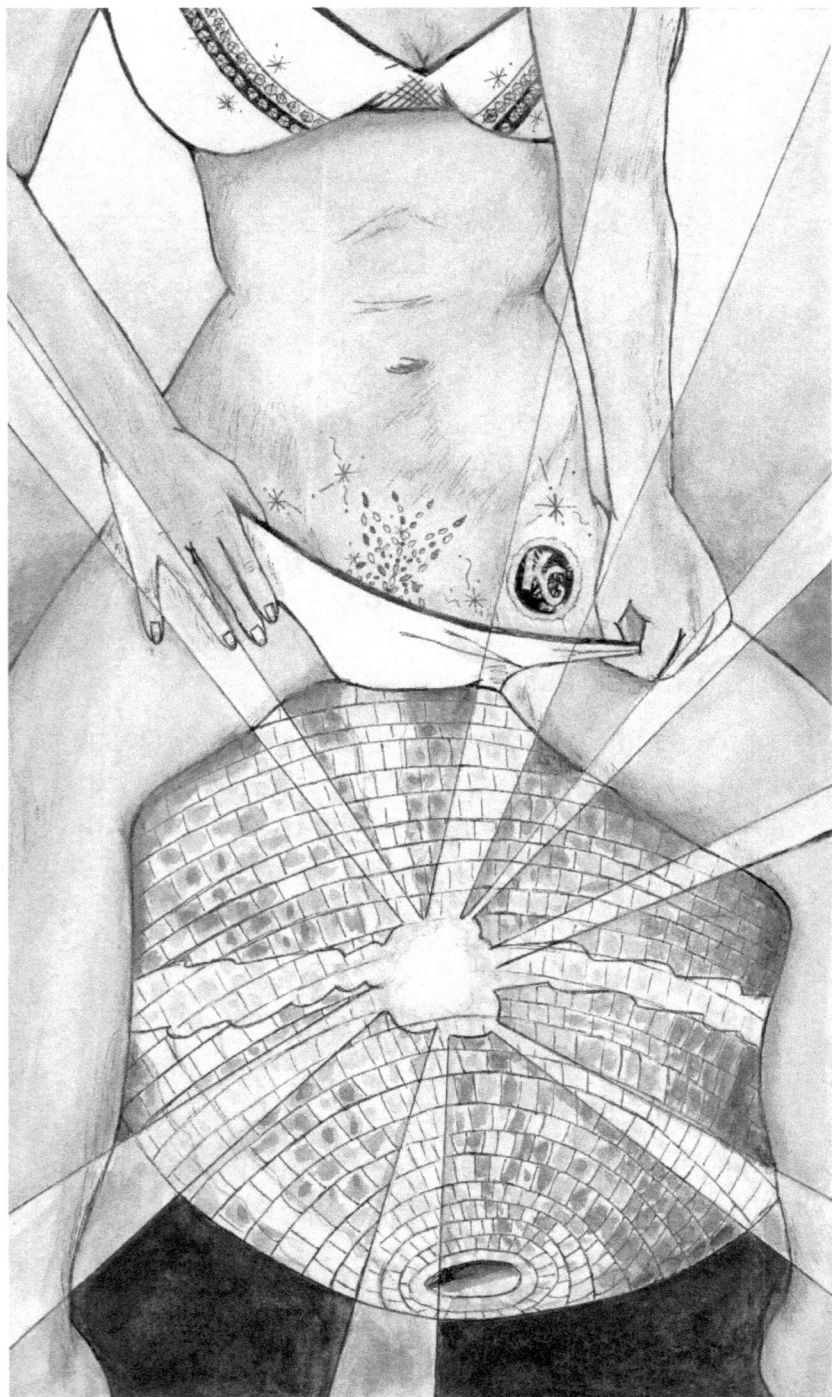

Bling Out Your Thing

Maybe you've heard of it, maybe you haven't. Either way, vajazzling is a sexy way to add a little bling to your thing. The world of vajazzling has butterflies, fireflies, sunbursts, and initials, just to name a few. You can practically vajazzle any body part.

Tiny Swarovski crystals are placed strategically on your body. Not only can you add bling to your newly-waxed vajayjay, but you can sparkle up your breasts, ankle, wrist, or hip, too.

I have vajazzled just about every body part there is. Initials are really popular. Imagine your man peeling back your panties to find his initials sparkling down below.

Designs come in all shapes and sizes: blues, purples, silvers, pinks... and when the light hits them, it's like a disco ball going off in your pants.

For the right price, I'll make any vagina look like an art gallery! You'll be the talk of the town when you sparkle and shine. We could even do your behind!

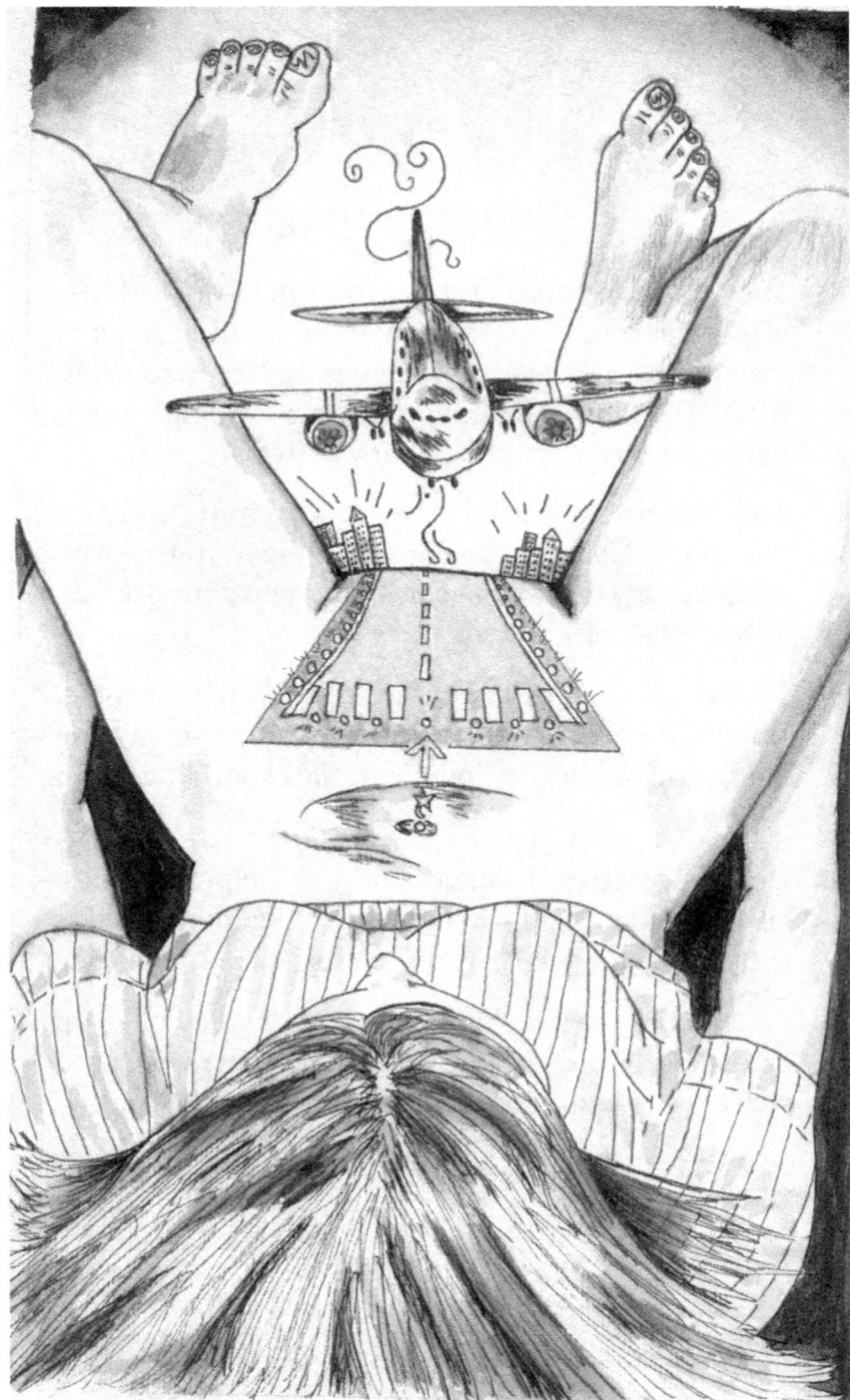

Coming in for a Landing

Roger – ready for takeoff! Small or large, some clients love the look of a good ol' classic landing strip. I mean really, why do we call it that? The only thing landing down there is your man's... well, you get the picture.

I get all kinds of requests: "Can you just leave it up top, but take everything else off?" Or "Maybe leave a trail from top to bottom?"

I've decided to change the name from *landing strip* to *racing stripe*. Who would know the difference? Maybe I can patent the racing stripe and people all over the world would have my famous stripe. Dream big, Kim, dream big!

I'm the professional bushwhacker, so I vote for that bush to be completely clean. The full Brazilian is just a few more tugs. The landing will be so much easier when the runway is clear.

The Half-Waxed

So the client lays on the table and I ask, "Have you ever been waxed before?"

The client answers, "No," so I ask about her tolerance for pain.

She replies, "I can handle pain pretty well."

"OK," I reply. "Let's get started."

Pull, pull, pull! Three pulls and she's out!

Bitch, you said you could take it, but now you're jumping off my table. Oh, hell no. Once you've entered the world of waxing, KG don't let no one leave half-waxed!

As if pleading for her life, she tells me she'll pay full price. No way, sugar plum. This shit's gotta go. We're finishing. Lay there and take it like a champ. You are 50% done. You're gonna love the end result.

Ten minutes, and I pull the final tush hairs. A hard day's work done, but remember:

Beauty is pain, people.

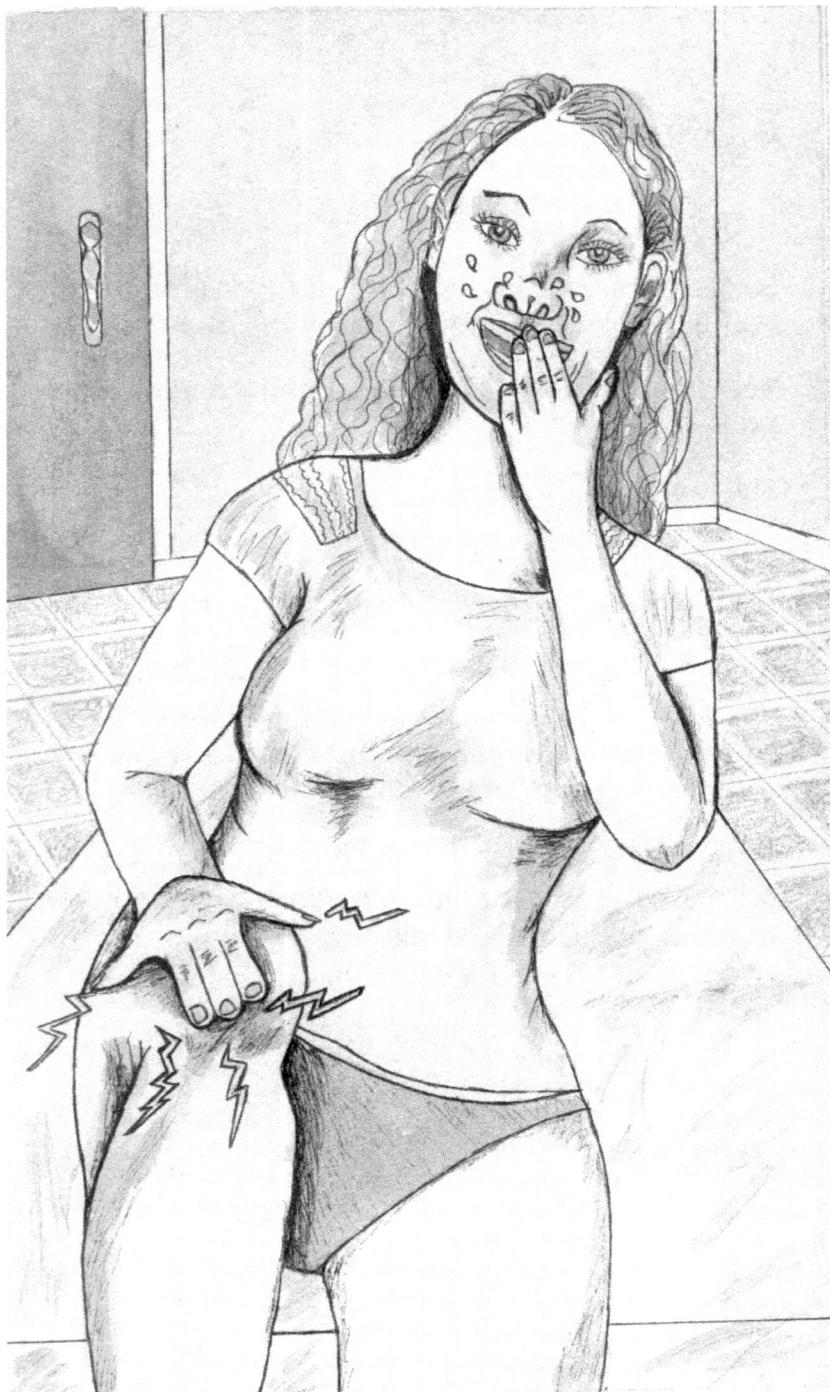

The Snorter

Why is it that when people get scared or nervous they laugh uncontrollably?

You're half laughing, half crying, begging for the waxing to stop, when all of a sudden Wilbur from *Charlotte's Web* makes his appearance — a sound I'd rather not discuss, but too embarrassing for me to pass up.

After the snorting starts, the laughter gets louder. Not only are you in pain, and embarrassed that your legs are spread open to a complete stranger, but now I don't know if I should wax ya or stuff an apple in your mouth and roast ya over a fire pit!

Get your ass off my bed and wee, wee, wee, all the way home. Snort! Snort!

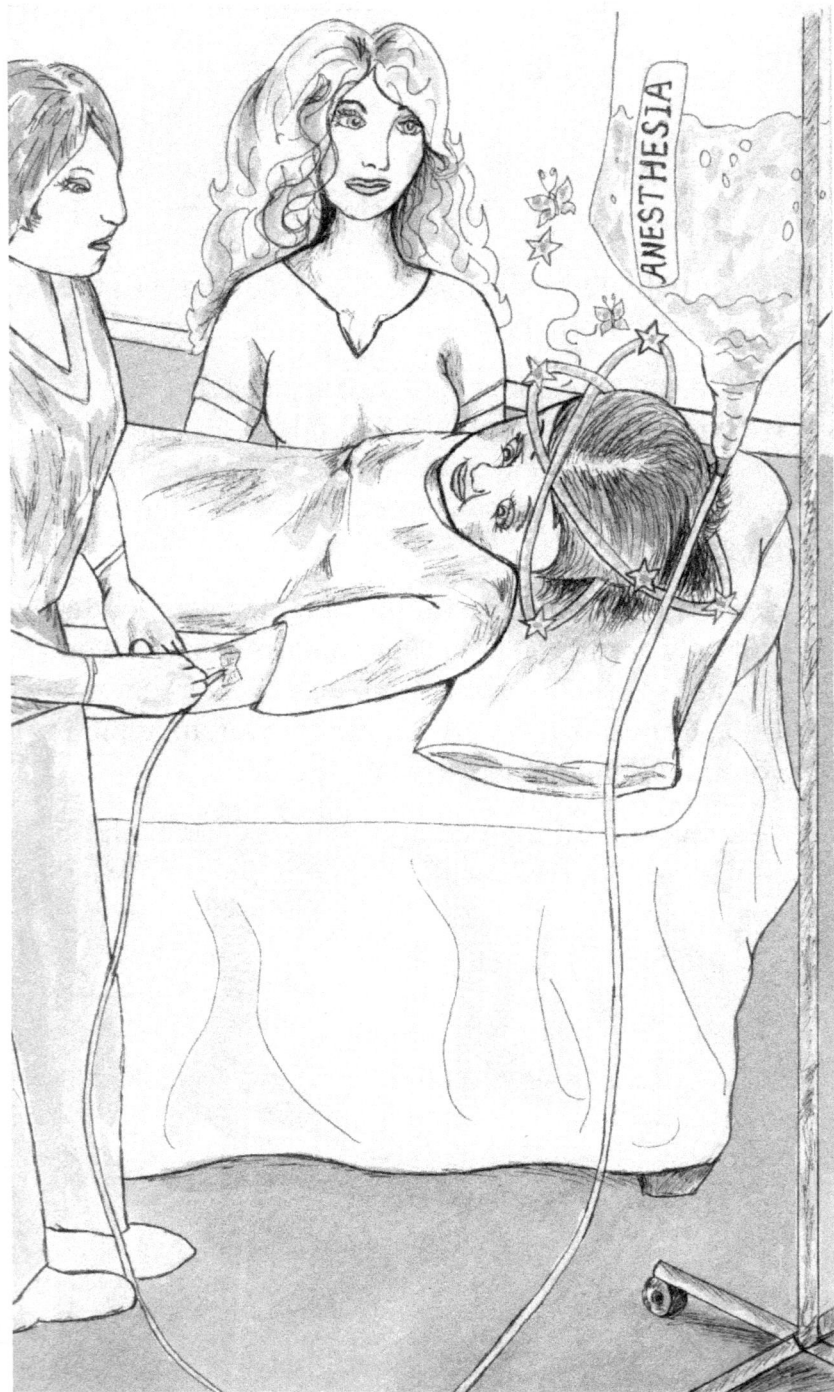

Is it Dumb to Numb?

People ask me all the time... can I get numbed so the wax doesn't hurt? Let me give you some advice. The best numbing agent in the world is getting a needle stuck in your arm by a nurse standing next to you saying that when you wake up, you won't remember a thing.

There are so many numbing agents out there, but really, do you think for one moment that you're not gonna feel anything? I mean, come on. It's hot wax! Hairs are being ripped right out of the small holes in your skin. Nice try, sweetie.

For you chicken shits out there, Lidocaine helps, but you have to apply it half an hour before you come in for doomsday. I also have an organic number that works for a few minutes, but no pain, no gain.

You want to be beautiful? Suck it up! It only hurts for like what, ten minutes? If you are that much of a pussy, then maybe your pussy isn't ready to be center stage.

Cougar Crotches

A client walks in and I do a double take. "Clean me up good today," she says. "I'm sure I'm going to get some tonight!"

The thrill of it all; this 60-something sexy woman is out on the prowl ready to pounce on whatever young prey comes her way.

She tells me that she just bought a new little black dress, nine-inch stilettos, and wants a clean crotch. She wants to be ready for the stud she takes home tonight.

At first I was like, "OMG, old wrinkly vagina. Who wants to hit that?" But then I thought about it and was like, "Damn, you go, girl!" I hope I can be that confident and sexy when I'm over the hill!

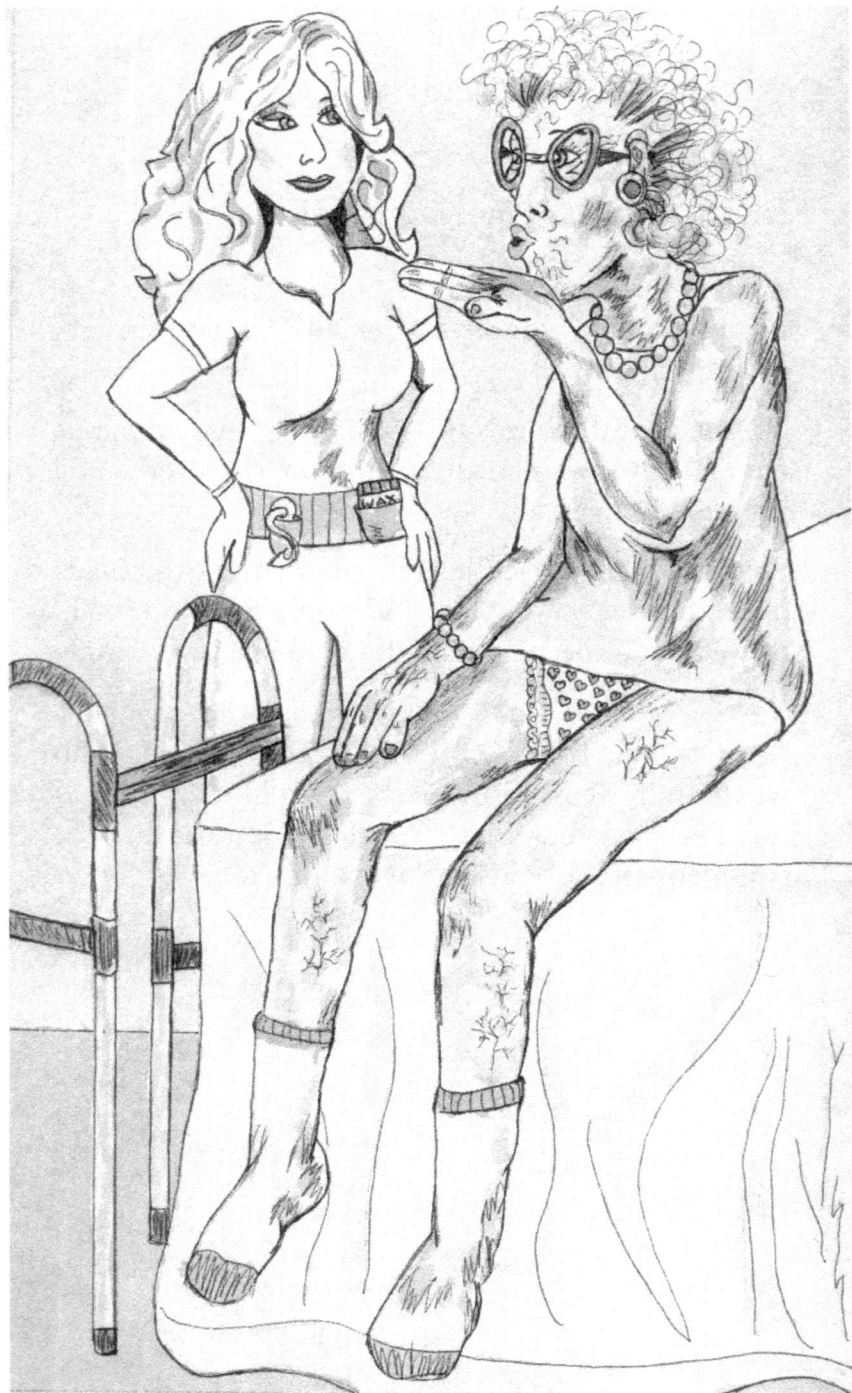

Retired and Horny

The name should have clued me in – Esther – but I didn't put two and two together before I saw her. You see them all the time... those silver-haired little old ladies who look so cute and innocent. Step into my arena and hear them roar!

She gets up on my table (with a little help since she has arthritis), and exclaims, "Seventy never felt so good! My mom would never have done this!" She wishes she'd started doing this years ago. She explains how her husband loves her skin being so clean and hairless.

"Now that we're both retired," she says, "we're like rabbits."

TMI, I think, but hey, good for her for being able to go at it like that at her age. She's lived a long life taking care of her husband, kids, and working a full time job for 40 years. If she wants to get a Brazilian wax and live life to the fullest, more power to her! Nobody wants a silver beaver.

Married with a Side Boo

She walks in and I ask, "So why are you getting waxed today? Got a getaway with your husband?"

The red-cheeked woman answers, "Well, kinda sorta." Then she adds in a whisper, "It's for my side boo."

"Really! I just saw you out last week with your husband and kids. Did you get a divorce in the last seven days?"

She pleads with me not to tell on her. What am I going to do? There's some sneaky shit going on up in here. Cue the Nelly song, *"It's getting hot in here... so take off all your clothes..."*

Of course I wanna know the down and dirty, so I ask where she's meeting him.

She explains that the rendezvous is with her multimillion-dollar lover downtown and he showers her with gifts, jewelry, and money. What more could a girl ask for? Some girls have all the luck.

As I go in for the next strip, I realize it's time for me to wake up from this dream. I need to get back to the reality of waxing this woman who's having sex with her husband, and a side boo, too.

Ho with a Fro

So you think you're cute coming in here all monkey-skirted up? Once you take those pants off, you ain't shit with that ridiculous fro popping out. I've seen some fros in my day, let me tell ya. The red-haired ones always get me. It's just like *poof* and Happy the Clown's fro pops out.

People, why do you wait so long? Who wants to see that down there? I sure as hell don't. I guess there are some guys out there who are into that sorta thing, but they're probably the ones who still live in their mother's basement playing video games.

Wake up! These people must live in the Stone Age. I'll be glad to use the clippers on that disgusting ho fro, or please, just get it all waxed off! I can't imagine how uncomfortable you are walking around with that gigantic jungle all day... itching and scratching and maneuvering to keep that bush from escaping your underpants.

Even if your man says he likes it, he probably doesn't. He just wants to get laid and avoid a fight. Don't be that ho with a fro, baby.

Sophisticated Bitch

Just because you're driving up to my shop in a Bentley, wearing a Chanel jacket, and carrying an $8,000 designer bag doesn't mean you don't grow hair like the rest of 'em.

Ever hear that phrase, "Everybody shits"? Well, same goes for pubic hair. Everybody's got it, no matter how rich or poor, fat or skinny, tan or pale. Just like everyone else, you have hair that needs to be removed. Trust me, the more sophisticated, the crazier they become once I get 'em on my table.

That snotty, reserved speech goes out the window when the first strip comes ripping off. The devil may wear Prada, but in my room, the sophisticated bitch bows down to my rules.

Don't be Farty for the Party

Yup. It happens. ALL THE TIME! Clients will come in all perfectly made up and styled like they're stepping out of a Hollywood magazine. They get up on my table and I start the wax. After a few pulls and some conversation about their fabulous lives, out comes the toots.

At first I think I'm hearing things, and maybe it was just a shift of the table or a squeak of my shoe on the floor. Then the smell hits me like a ton of bricks. Nope, I say, that was definitely a fart.

While your ass cheeks are spread, I get it right in my face. A puff of pure gas comes straight at me. Some people laugh and apologize. Others just ignore it and act like it didn't happen. Still others apologize and turn beet red all embarrassed.

We all fart. I get it. But please try and hold it in until I'm done. If you absolutely can't, at least warn me, so I can get the hell out of the way. I'll need to light a candle to mask the stench.

Don't Pee on Me!

You might think this doesn't happen because I deal with grown adults on a daily basis, but believe me, I've been sprinkled during a waxing session.

I don't know if it's the feeling of the hot wax, or the pressure on your pubic bone when I pull the strips, but all of a sudden the Hoover Dam opens up. Now granted, this doesn't happen all the time, but it's happened more than once and was shocking enough to scar me for life.

The last thing I want or need is your pee on my hands or all over my table. If you have a weak or sensitive bladder, go to the bathroom before we get started. Most places have a restroom you can use.

At least warn me that you're going to tinkle, even if it's just a sprinkle! I'll be able to get out of the way and grab you a Depends coupon, since apparently you are in desperate need of some diapers.

Elephant Lips

Elephant lips, uneven Stevens, long lips, you name it. I've seen them all. Not that a vagina is ever pretty, but there are some that are normal and then there are others that just plain look like they're from outer space.

I have to contain my shock when I uncover what's beneath that bush—long lips flapping in the wind. I mean, you could braid that shit, some of them are so long. How do you walk around all day with those things swinging in the breeze? You almost would need to roll them up and tuck them in.

It's like that song... "Do your lips hang low? Do they wobble to and fro? Can you tie 'em in a knot? Can you tie 'em in a bow?" Some people probably could throw them over their shoulders!

Find a good plastic surgeon and get that shit taken care of.

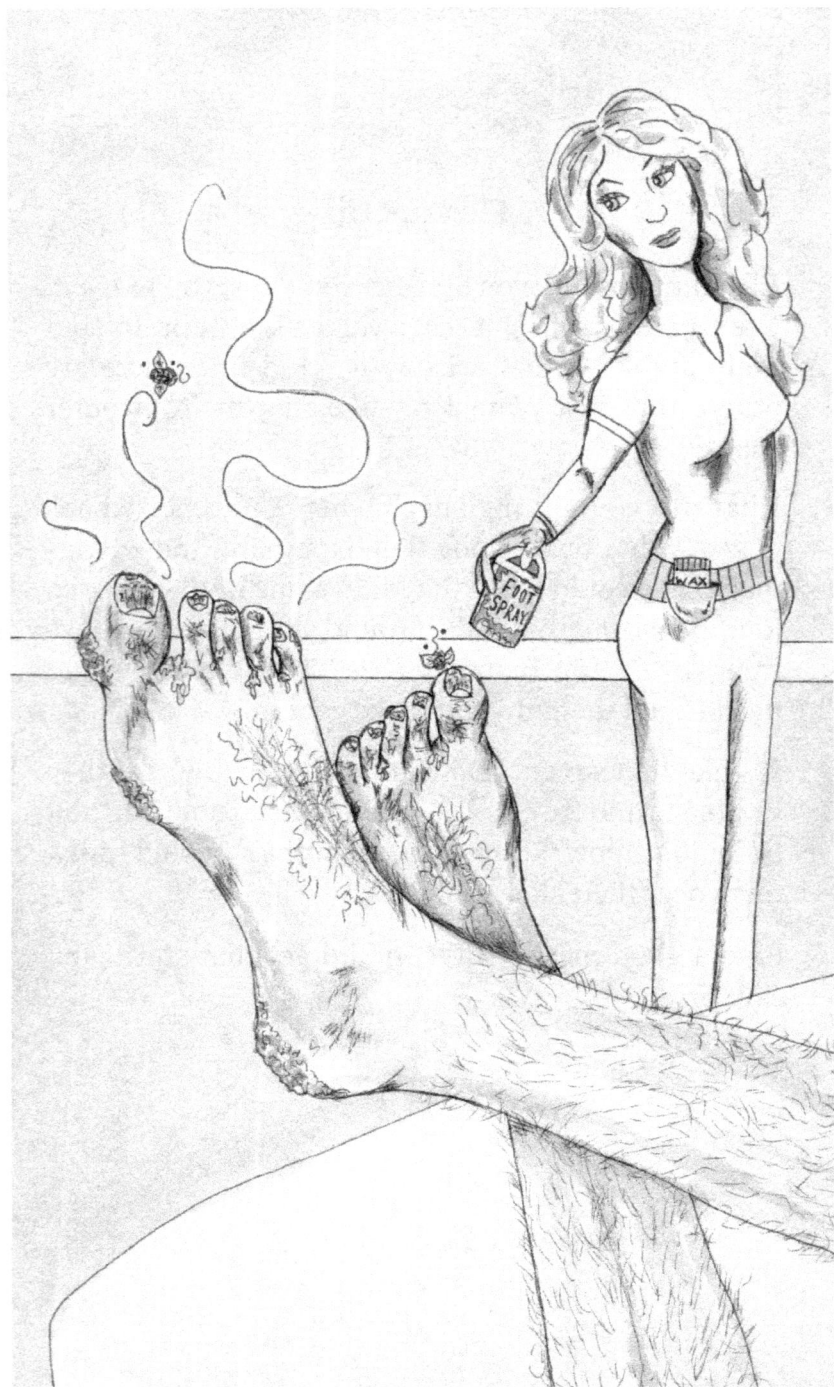

Funky Feet

Smelly feet...

stinky feet...

gnarly toes...

...your waxer knows!

Screamers and Criers

Stop the madness. You need not scream bloody murder like a woman in the sixteenth hour of labor without an epidural. It's not that serious.

The waiting clients didn't know to pack earplugs. They've been listening to you scream for fifteen minutes now, like there's a gun pointed at your head.

I swear, once a month I should sponsor a "loudest screamer contest." The winner would receive a starring role in the next horror flick for their blood curdling screams.

The echo gets louder with every pull and tweeze. Brazilians aren't exactly pain free—I agree. Five to fifteen minutes is all I need. Save the drama for your mama.

And crying? Child, please. Don't get me started.

Momma's Girl

If Mommy has to come and hold your hand during your waxing, you shouldn't be making an appointment in the first place.

A twenty-something bride-to-be comes in with her mom. She's already crying and shaking in anticipation of what's to come. The second I place a stick of warm wax on her pet beaver, she's tries to escape.

I hadn't even made the first pull yet. Her mom is like, "Honey, it's gonna be okay. Don't worry, everything's gonna be just fine."

Okay...

I'm like, "Oh my God. Puh-lease. Gag me with a spoon." But I had to remain professional and prepare her for what's to come.

Riiiippp... off came enough hair to insulate an Alaskan stripper.

She shrieked and rolled over on her side. "Mommy," she sobbed. "Do I have to finish?"

I could not believe this was actually happening. If your wedding's in a week and you can't handle a simple Brazilian... *then girlfriend*, you don't need to be getting married.

To my surprise, she decided to continue, with some coaxing from mommy. I mean seriously. Patchy pubes are not in style.

It literally took 45 minutes of screams, tears, and hugs from mom to get her through this crazy wax. I was damn glad when that shit was all over.

She left my room looking like she'd just had wild sex with a heavyweight champ. Farewell, mommy dearest, and to the bare-skinned bridezilla.

P.S. Seriously? Two bucks?? Obviously your mommy didn't teach you anything... especially how to tip.

The Bum: To Wax or Not to Wax?

That is the Question.

No one wants to talk about it or admit it, but we've all got it. Yup, ass hair. You think it's gross and wish it wasn't there. Hello, get it waxed.

I have women ask me all the time, "Do a lot of people get that done?"

I answer, "What? The shrubs sticking outta your ass? Shut up and get those legs in the air, cause I'm coming in!"

A clean bum is a happy bum. Your first shit after de-hairing that ass, you'll be sending me a thank you card.

One word of advice though. Wipe that rump after you dump. No one wants to see the remnants of diarrhea or dookie where the light don't shine.

I'm a waxer, not a wiper.

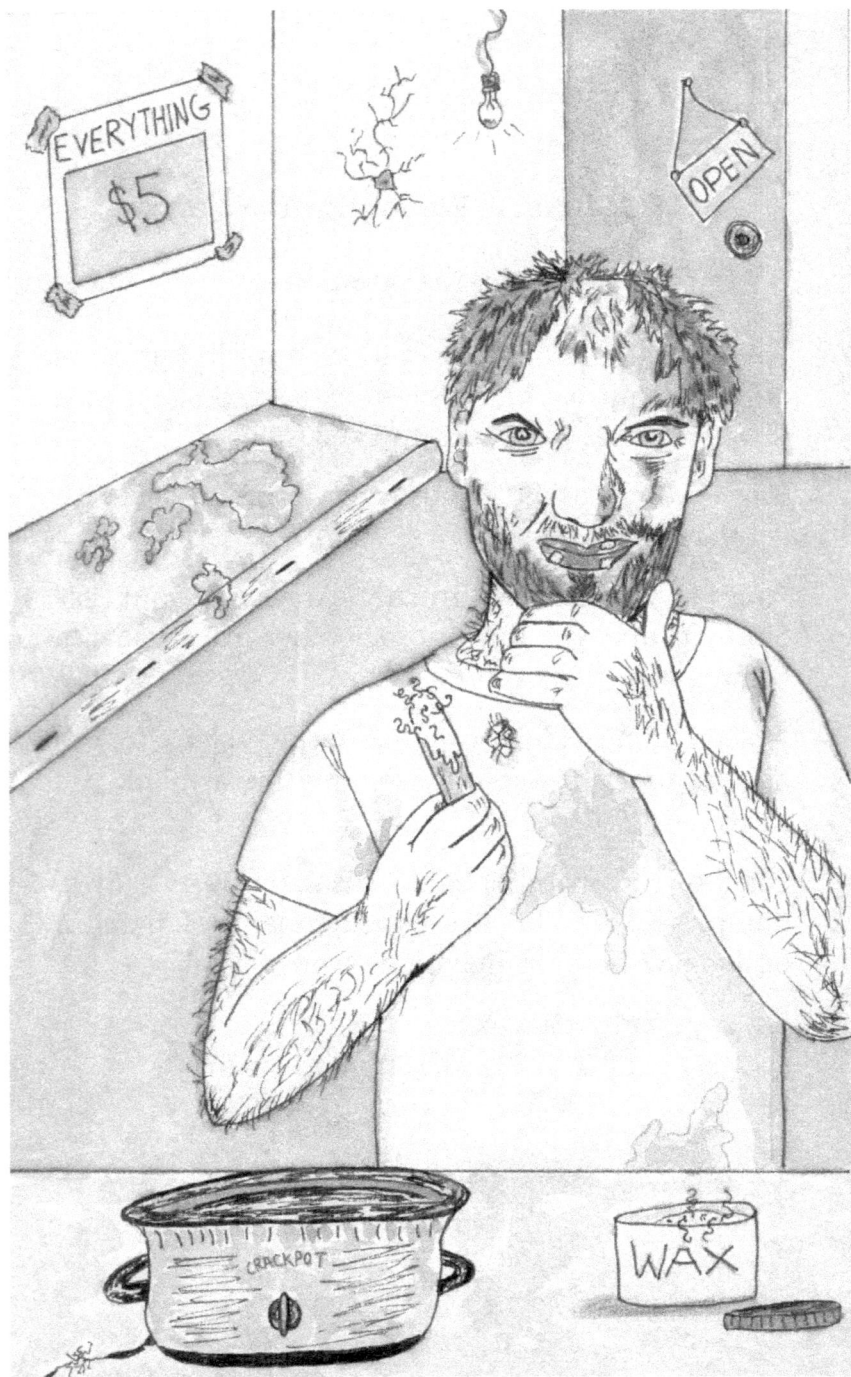

I'd Rather be Maced than have Crotch on My Face

"What?" you say to yourself. What the hell is this crazy bitch talking about?

This is the 21st century. There's herpes, AIDS, crabs, warts, and all kinds of shit lurking around.

Think about it. You go to get your upper lip waxed and the waxer dips the same stick that just waxed the hairy balls of the guy who left before you. Wake up and smell the jock itch, people!

Seriously, you wouldn't want someone to rub their dirty panties on your face, would you? (Well... maybe some people out there would, but that's a whole other book.)

When getting waxed, tell that esthetician, "No double dipping!"

How many crotches do you want on your face today? Hell to the N-O!

Where's the Vajayjay?

Oh my! Give me a minute to find my goggles, gloves, and industrial strength chain saw. I must cut down that bush, and trim those overgrown hedges.

Wow. I've seen some shit in my day, but the moment some of you pull your underwear down, I feel like I need to consult with Philly's best landscaper. Guess you haven't done anything with that crotch hair since you were a teenager, huh?

Does that bush have a pulse? Damn, for a hot minute there I thought that thing was gonna come alive.

I seriously had to dive in with both hands to excavate that vagina. Warn me next time before you unleash the beast.

The Half-Ton Waxer

Just to let you know, I'm not what you would call a petite girl. I can definitely handle some chub.

But reeeaaaalllly, when I have to use two beds for one body, and recruit a crew of construction workers to hold up your stomach, I think it's gone waaay too far.

My brow is sweaty and I'm getting the feeling it's going to be a marathon session here. How in the world am I going to fit this 500-pound sumo giant on my table? We've got a quadruple here, and we've got to make it fit on a single! You do the math.

I need to lift some weights and get a trainer before I attempt waxing this one. By the time I pull up the third stomach roll, I already need a break.

After going through the folds and rolls, I finally get to the privates that haven't seen the light of day in decades. I look like a friggin' circus act trying to hold up fifty pounds of pure abdomen with my elbow.

Upon completion, I'm exhausted and frail. Call the next clients: "Sorry, gotta bail!"

Is it a Boy or a Girl?

Oh, hell no. What the F@%! is that? The client comes in, lays on the table. I get ready to wax. Do you have elephantitis of the clit, or is that a penis?

I'm not sure how to charge for this. What the hell happened down there? Was there some kind of accident at the bris you're not telling me about? How am I supposed to wax that thing? Should I guess? Is there some kind of poll that gives a majority vote?

How do you pee out of that thing? It looks like the elephant man came back from the grave. I really am not sure what to do with that vapenis. Please let me know because I'm very confused.

This was not covered in waxing school! I do the best I can, but pull your pants up. You're at the wrong place. The plastic surgeon's office is down the hall.

Hold the Mayo

Warning. Put down your sandwich because you're gonna lose your appetite after this one.

A client comes in... and I don't mean to brag... but I guess my hotness turned her on. Either that or she was super sensitive and got aroused as soon as my glove touched her skin. Whatever the reason, it was like a jar of Hellman's exploded all over me and my table.

After every pull I was wiping that shit up. I couldn't believe what was happening. If I was a fertilization doctor, I could put that spunk in a vial and freeze it. I'd be a millionaire. But wait, that's man-jizz... just sayin'.

Open the lip, apply the wax, lay the strip on, and uh oh... need to call maid service, cuz that white stuff just splattered all over my room. Save that creamy mess for the bedroom, not the wax room.

Herpes Ho (Holy STD, Batman!)

What was it that Eddie Murphy said in *Delirious*? "Herpes. You carry that shit around like luggage."

It surprised me the first time I saw it... the scabby, scaly skin staring up at me. Now, I've seen so many cases I'm immune to it.

Whatever. You've got the herpes. Accept it, own it, get over it. I could give a shit. I'm just here to remove your hair, so don't lie to me.

People come in and tell me not to mind the "dry skin" down there. Try to deny... I will catch you with my super eye!

I especially love when they ask, "Does my skin look irritated?"

Ummm, yeah. You have herpes, ho. And I'm waxing hair surrounded by those oozing sores. I'm not a doctor, and I don't need a degree to know you have "that thang."

It's like a science project down there. I don't need an encyclopedia to figure out what that shit is. I'm definitely gonna triple-glove up for this one.

This sore-infested bitch just keeps jabbering away like she thinks it's no big deal. A few pulls, and the warts and pimples appear. Wow. That's some nasty ass shit.

True. I tried to take cover and dive under the table when that white, puss-filled shit hit me right in the face. "Gag me with a spoon." I wiped my cheeks with my forearm, trying not to freak out.

You really need to see a doctor because you've got some serious shit going on down there. This is one case where having a giant bush is better than being waxed.

Soup to Nuts

Now it's time to focus on those male parts. I get them all—young, old, straight and gay. Just to give you a little hint... manscaping is a necessity. I love my teddy, but I mean, really ladies, who feels like sleeping with a hairy bear?

It's hilarious. These big tough macho men can't take the pain like women can. I love causing a man to cry and scream. There's something so powerful about that.

Whether the pubic area, chest, back or stomach, it turns into a scene from *Forty-Year-Old Virgin*. Except I don't give them time to yell, "Kelly Clarkson!"

Embarrassed and ashamed because they can't take the pain, that deep voice morphs into a high-pitched girlish scream.

I lie and pretend I feel bad, but in my head I'm like, *"Bitch, shut up and take it like a man!"* When you ordered off the menu from soup to nuts, you missed the fine print... it's back, crack and sack, pal!

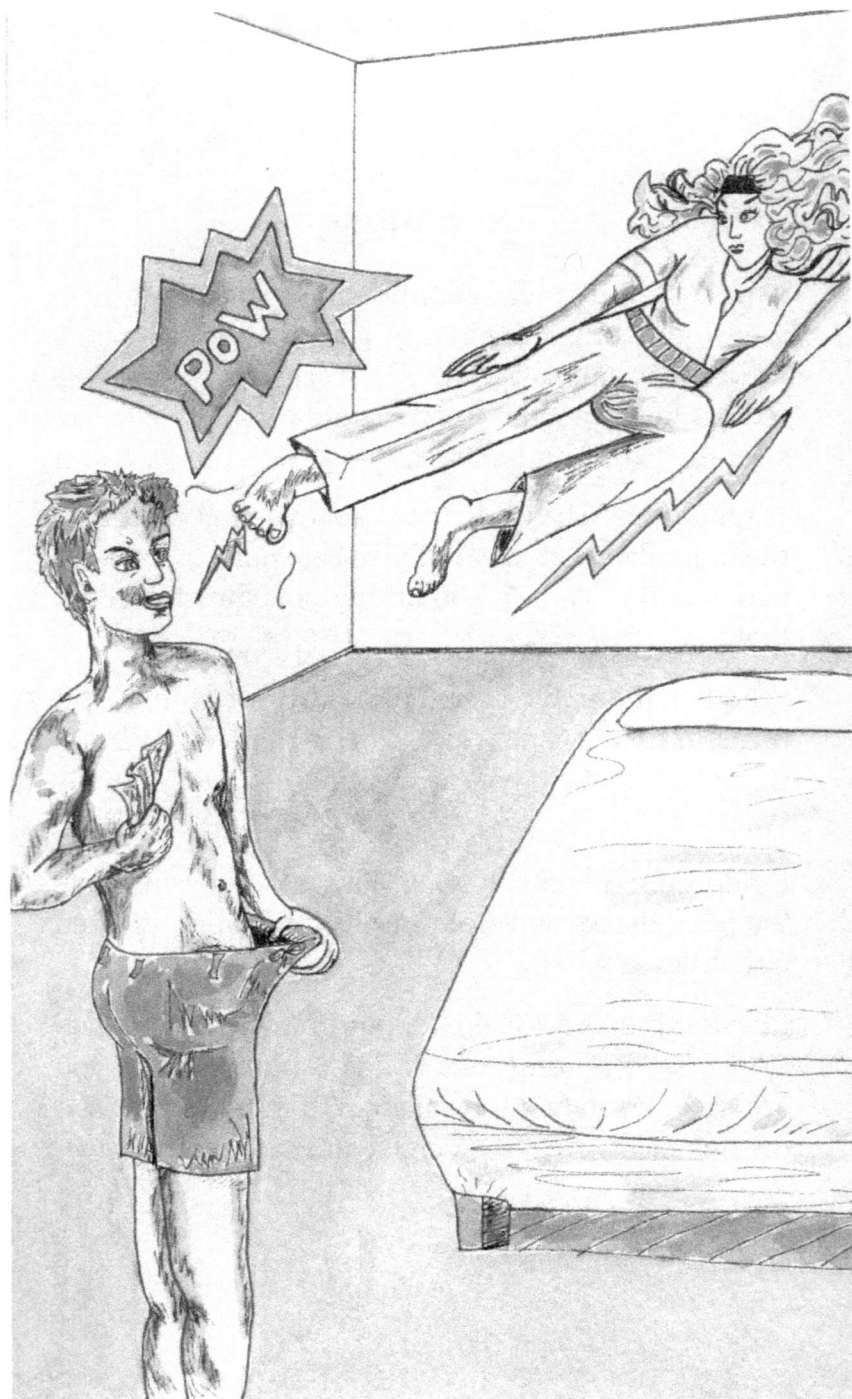

This is Not Happy Ending Time

You guys, you're so funny. The wind can blow a certain way, and oops... Pop goes the weasel! This is a wax, not a happy ending.

If you have no self-control, check the magazine rack, Jack. The men's room is the last door on the left.

I guess it's human nature but you know I'm not a masseuse or a call girl, so leave your hard-on for someone who cares.

When it happens, I calmly say, "Sir, here's a paper towel. When you are done, call me back in the room. I'll be waiting outside the door." No one wants to see that shit today.

It doesn't turn me on and I'm not gonna help you with that situation, so let's see how excited you are when I make my first pull. I'm sure you won't get turned on when a hundred hair follicles get yanked out of your most sensitive area one at a time.

You'll go from hard as a rock to limp dick Willy in like one second. Don't play with a girl with hot wax who likes to rhyme... Guys, this is not happy ending time!

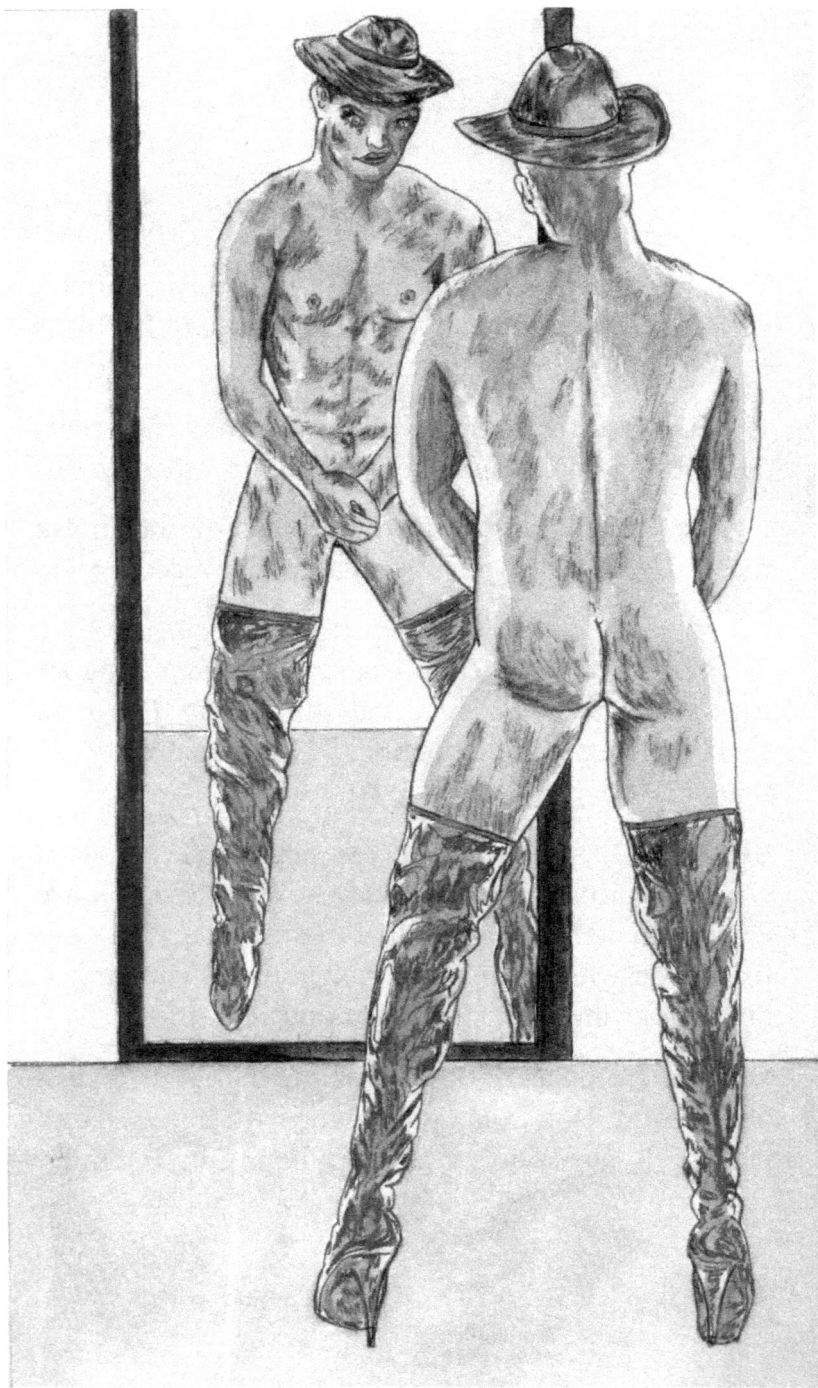

Queen with Means

Panic-stricken, he races into my salon. He's got a hot date tonight with a fresh young stud.

"Girl, you and my momma are the only two women I trust with these family jewels."

He's naked and ready, even before I can ask him to strip. Never crying, not once a scream or hesitation, this boy can't wait to tell me about the leopard-print mini-dress he might wear tonight.

From head to toe, he wants perfection. Not a hair left on his body, except for that platinum-blonde wig he just dropped off to be groomed.

We finish the last strip. He jumps up and can't wait to look in the mirror. Red lips, trim hips, standing naked in those six-inch stiletto heels, he's tall and lean, now completely clean. My favorite client... the queen with means.

Kim's Guidelines for a Happy Waxing Relationship

Before you go to the salon, follow these simple steps to make the experience better for both you and your waxer:

1. Wipe your ass.

2. Wipe your ass AGAIN.

3. Repeat steps 1 and 2.

4. Seriously – make sure you clean your ass.

5. If you're on the rag, clean yourself up and put in a fresh tampon.

6. If you know it's funky down there, wash yourself before you go, or at least clean up with a flushable wipe.

7. If you are one of those big-bushed women, warn your waxer so they know to get the hedge trimmers out.

8. If it's your first time getting waxed, explain this to your waxer. The process will go much smoother if they know you're a virgin.

9. Ask your waxer if they double dip their sticks. If they say yes, get the hell out of there so you don't get some kind of nasty infection or STD.

10. Ask your waxer if he/she is licensed, qualified, and insured. If they say no or look at you like you have six heads, pull your pants up and get the hell out of there.

11. No girly squirts or hard-ons. Do your thing before you get there, and if you are getting turned on, think about something else so you don't look like a weirdo.

12. Get a pedicure and clean your feet before you get waxed. If you can't handle that, at least wear socks.

About the Author

Kim Gider is an award-winning licensed esthetician and the owner of *Salon and Spa by Kimberly Gider* in Conshohocken, Pennsylvania.

To learn more or
book your appointment today,
visit: kimberlygider.com

Salon and Spa by Kimberly Gider
902-904 Fayette Street, Conshohocken, PA 19428